Square Foot Gardening Guide

A simple guide on everything you need to know for successful square foot gardening

Table of Contents

Introduction iv

Chapter 1 - Square Foot Gardening: Meaning, Basics, and Benefits 1

Chapter 2 - Getting Started 5

Chapter 3 - Your Soil 9

Chapter 4 - Your Plants 12

In growing runner plants, use strong frames with mesh. Make the area for root crops a little higher to gain maximum depth. 15

Chapter 5 - Proper Caring and Maintenance 19

Conclusion 22

Introduction

I want to thank you and congratulate you for downloading the book, *"Square Foot Gardening Guide"*.

This book contains helpful information about square foot gardening, what it is, and everything you need to know to get started.

Square foot gardening is a great new method of gardening, that further expands on the raised bed gardening method. Through dividing the garden bed in to different areas, you can achieve better growth, clear division of plants, and get the same gardening results in less time!

Through this book you will learn how to construct your very own square foot garden, make your own compost, choose the right plants, and care for your garden!

There are a range of plants that your can grow using a square foot garden, with much less effort than a traditional garden. Furthe`r on in this book, you will be provided with a sample garden plan that will give you suggestions on which plants to grow, and where to place them.

This book will also explain to you advanced tips and techniques that will help you successfully start your own square foot garden, and keep it healthy!

Good luck on your gardening journey, I wish you all the best and hope this book can be of some service to you!

Thanks again for downloading this book, I hope you enjoy it!

Chapter 1 - Square Foot Gardening: Meaning, Basics, and Benefits

The emergence of Square Foot Gardening or SFG was made possible and was popularized by Mel Bartholomew. The planting method came to be in response to the incompetence of conventional gardening. The aim is to create a trouble-free and easy to maintain garden using raised beds. With this method, you don't need to spend as much time attending to your garden and you will still get fresh produce.

Mel Bartholomew is an engineer with a passion for gardening and he applied his analytical skills to his hobby. It solved the problems that he encountered while pursuing his hobby. He found out that the typical gardener spends long hours of weeding the gaps that separate the long rows. He realized that eliminating the rows and using raised beds enclosed in frame can improve gardening. It can also cut the amount of time that a gardener should spend in maintaining and caring for the garden. The added square grid on top of the bed makes it easy to rotate the crops. The grid structure he created provides the needed space between the crops.

In a nutshell, all you need is to build a frame for your SFG, fill it with soil, and top it with the grid and you are ready to plant. It is not hard to start a square foot garden and it is a worthwhile hobby that you and your family will enjoy.

The Basics of Square Foot Gardening

The ideal area for SFG is four feet by four feet area for planting. Always think in squares and remove gardening in rows from your mind. It also needs a two to three feet wide gap between the beds to serve as your path walk.

The box frame that will contain your garden should be no wider than four feet. The materials for the box can be wood, cinder blocks, or vinyl. While a frame doesn't need a bottom or a cover, lining the frame with weed cloth at the bottom can make a big difference.

Make sure to form aisles if you want to build more than a single square foot garden. The gap between the boxed gardens should measure two to three feet.

Prepare the grid and put it on top of the soil. It will divide the box to make rotation easier. The grid partitions the box into one foot square. If you have four feet by four feet box, then you will need a grid with sixteen squares.

In SFG, all you need to do is reach in when you tend to your plants. It is important to keep the width at four feet wide and nothing more. It would be hard to maintain the garden if it goes beyond the four feet width. If it goes beyond the suggested max width, you may need to step on the soil which defies the purpose of having a square foot garden.

Important Things to Take Note in the SFG System

Unlike the usual method in gardening, SFG uses raised beds enclosed by a frame. It is important to follow the four feet width to avoid facing trouble. You can have as many beds as you like as long as they have two or three feet wide aisle between each bed or frame.

You can even arrange the beds to follow a certain design if you want something that can also provide aesthetic appeal.

The depth of the beds should be between six and twelve inches which will provide the rich nutrients that the plants need. It can also provide a good drainage.

The soil mix must have equal portions of peat moss, compost, and vermiculite. In other words your soil composition must be one third peat moss, one third compost, and one third vermiculite. Starting with such mixture can ensure a weed-free garden. It also has the ability to retain water and provide a soil that is full of nutrients.

You should not walk on the soil, and that is the reason for the four feet max width. If you will be able to reach your plants without trouble, allowing you to tend to your plants without walking on the soil.

The Benefits, Advantages, and Disadvantages of SFG

There are many benefits and advantages that SFG can provide such as less weeding or none at all; you will be able to conserve water; it offers shade to companion plants; it gives fresh and organic produce; and it can also be a stress buster.

Children are especially fond of the idea of growing things with their own hands. SFG is considered a small garden that can give you and your children a quality activity to do together. You will be able to teach them how to be responsible, caring, patient, and frugal. At the same time, they can have a lot of fun seeing their plants grow!

SFG is also good for people who experience difficulty in bending over due to aging, illness, and other factors that may limit their range of motion.

It can become a good project for the entire community or any organization that you are affiliated with.

Many SFG enthusiasts claim that the square foot garden can provide more produce, doesn't need too much soil and water, and it only needs minutes of your time for its care and maintenance. At a glance, SFG has many advantages over the conventional method of gardening.

Like any gardening method however, SFG also has its share of disadvantages. You may find that the square foot gardening method can be quite expensive. The materials for the frame are quite costly as well as the soil mixture. It may seem this way at first, but in the long run the beds will continue to give quality produce, and can be reused again and again. The soil will make sure that your plants grow without issue, and this method of gardening will also save you time!

Now that you know what square foot gardening is, the benefits, and the basics in putting up a square foot garden, it's time to get started.

Chapter 2 - Getting Started

Starting a square foot gardening is not as hard as it may seem. It can provide a good opportunity to gather everyone in the family and spend some quality time together. It can also turn out to be one of your successful community projects. As you will find, the effort is definitely worthwhile!

The Layout and Frame

Although SFG can be expensive, there are ways to save some money for your frame. You can use simple and inexpensive lumber to build your frame. The lumber may be scrap or new. You need two-inch thick wood that you can turn into a four feet by four feet planting area. So the planks need to be approximately 2 inches thick, 48 inches long, and 12 inches deep.

If you are not so particular about the initial expense and want something to last for a long time, then get cedar. It won't rot right away and it is suitable to house your raised bed. If you are tight on the budget, then pine will do. You can use scrap wood for your frame, as long as it is around the right size. Other materials you can use for the frame are cinder block and vinyl.

The preferred size of your frame is four feet by four feet, but you can also use two by four. Keep in mind that the maximum width should only be four feet. The frame should be sturdy enough to hold the amount of dirt that you will put in later.

It is best to build a box that has a depth between six and twelve inches. If you are uncertain about the kind of plants you will put, it is best to choose the twelve-inch depth. Make sure to get the correct measurement before cutting your wood.

After making your frame, you can line the bottom part with weed cloth before adding in your soil.

Your Garden Aisles

If you want to have more than one raised bed in a box, then you need to have two or three feet wide walkways or path walks between the boxed gardens.

Aisles can be made from mulch, brick, colored stones, pebbles, grass, or any material that will look great with your garden design.

The Soil for your Garden

It may seem practical to just dig up some soil from your yard and put it in your square foot garden, but its not. Your "local soil" may come with pest and disease that will ruin your plants in the end.

As previously mentioned, it's best to have equal parts of compost, peat moss, and vermiculite of one third each. Before filling your box or boxes with soil, make sure to put your box or boxes in the exact space or location that you intend to use them. Otherwise you will have a hard time moving your box or boxes. Plan everything first before proceeding with your project. Take note that there are plants that love the sunshine and there are others that prefer the shade. Research your plants, and decide which square foot each will be planted it, and where the box will be placed. It is also advisable to choose a level spot to ensure uniform drainage.

The Grid

You need to put a grid above each frame and secure it in a permanent spot. It serves as the partition that separates the soil into squares of one square foot each. The grid is the unique feature in SFG that handles the whole system with efficiency.

Care, Selection, and Planting

You can put one, four, nine, or sixteen plants per square or grid depending on the size of the plant when it matures. Put one plant in the square if it is a large one, four if the plant is a medium one, nine or sixteen for small plants. If you want to grow runner plants like peas, you will need a strong frame with string or mesh.

You can also choose to cover your beds for a few weeks with clear plastic prior to planting if you want to make sure that weeds will not invade your garden later. The plastic cover will warm the soil and will force weed sprouts to come out. You can remove them right away and save your plants some trouble.

In planting your seeds, make a shallow hole using your finger and drop two or three seeds in the hole. Cover the hole with soil and make sure not to pack too much soil heavily on top. Once the seeds begin to sprout, preserve the good ones and snip off the bad ones. You can store your extra seeds in a cool and dry area like your refrigerator and use them when needed. With SFG, you must remember not to over-plant.

Watering your Plants

In watering your plants, make sure to water the root area only. Water your plants often during the first few days and on dry days that are hot. Remember to research your plants and determine how often they need to be watered.

Look for tell-tale signs such as the color of leaves to determine if they need more or less watering.

Harvesting

Once a particular square in your boxed garden is ready for harvesting, make sure to harvest continually. Try and keep your grid full of plants, and rotate them as the season's progress.

By keeping your garden full, you can provide you and your family with fresh produce all year round, without too much effort, and in only a small space!

Chapter 3 - Your Soil

It is important to keep the ideal soil mixture in mind and that is equal parts of compost, vermiculite, and peat moss. Mix them well and your plants will sure to grow healthy and strong. Because your SFG is contained, you don't need to continually improve the soil because the soil mixture you have won't change. All you need to do is water the plants, remove dead leaves and branches, and harvest your produce.

It can be expensive to buy compost, but the good news is that you can make one from some of the biodegradable wastes in your home. You need to add compost before planting a different and new crop each time a certain crop leaves the square vacant.

You can make your own compost bin out of ordinary containers, buy a ready made one, or make one in your yard with some help from wood scraps and chicken wire.

Your Compost Bin

Making a compost bin out of wood scraps and chicken wire is easy. Choose the area in your yard where you would like to put your open compost bin. Put up four poles to make a square that is big enough to hold your compost then enclose it (sides only) with chicken wire. Secure the chicken wire to the wood scrap pole using nails. All you need now are the things that you will put in your compost bin.

If you would like to use plastic containers for your compost bin, then you need to pick a big enough container with lid. Drill some holes in the sides of the container as well as the bottom. Add some soil inside the bin according to the amount of compost that you desire to have. Put some shredded paper first such as newspaper and scratch papers before adding the permitted things to throw in.

There are ready made compost bins that you can buy from stores, but you can save some cash if you make your own bin.

Now that you have your own compost bin, it is time to gather the materials to throw in.

Things to Throw In and Things That You Should Not

When people hear about making your own compost, the first thing that usually comes to their mind is how smelly it will be. However, your compost won't smell badly if you are careful about the things you throw in your bin.

You can put trimmings or peelings of vegetables and fruits in your compost bin as well as eggshells, tea bags, cardboard, coffee grounds as well as filters, pieces of newspaper, shells of nuts, grass clippings, yard trimmings, paper, leaves, wood chips including sawdust, wool rags, cotton fibers, hair, dead houseplants without illness, lint from dryers and vacuum cleaners, hay, fur, and ashes.

Be careful not throw in charcoal ash or coal in your compost bin. Also avoid dairy products like yogurt, milk, egg white or yolk, and butter; twigs or leaves of a black walnut tree; fats including grease, oil, and lard; fish bones; meat scraps; plants with disease; pet wastes; and yard trimmings treated with chemicals. The said things may harm you and your loved ones, invite pests, and give off a foul smell.

Keep in mind to always look after your pile and throw only the permitted things in the bin. A well managed bin will not give off unpleasant odor. Sometimes you can also use worm castings compost, manure, or green waste.

Make sure to maintain the balance between the wet and dry things that you put in your compost bin to keep the unpleasant odor at bay. Don't forget to mix or turn your pile at least once a week. You may need to add scoops of new soil. Your compost will be ready in a few weeks.

Chapter 4 - Your Plants

In choosing your plants, makes sure to pick the ones that you and your family will enjoy the most. It is also wise to include one or two plants that can help control pests.

Sample List of Plants to Get you Going

You will find below a list of plants and their corresponding number per square.

PLANT	NO. PER SQUARE
Winter Squash	1
Broccoli	1
Zucchini	1
Strawberry	1
Okra	1
Hot Pepper	1
Peppers	1
Melon	1
Bok Choi	1
Brussels Sprouts	1
Cabbage	1

Cauliflower	1
Chive	1
Eggplant	1
Oregano	1
Rosemary	1
Pumpkin	1
Sage	1
Summer Squash	1
Sweet Potatoes	1
Kale	4
Garlic	4
Kohlrabi	4
Head Lettuce	4
Potatoes	4
Fennel	4
Beans	4
Corn	4
Cucumber	4
Parsley	4
Rutabaga	4
Basil	4

Swiss Chard	4
Thyme	4
Celery	4
Calendula	4
Marigold	4
Leeks	9
Onion	9
Turnip	9
Spinach	9
Peas	9
Dill	9
Beats	9
Parsnips	9
Cilantro	9
Carrots	16
Leaf Lettuce	16
Radish	16
Arugula	16

Some plants like spinach, chard, kale, and many variety of lettuce can tolerate shade. There are also plants that love the sun so much like basil, chives, fennel, thyme, garlic, oregano, green beans, peppers, peas, beets, radish, tomato, squash, and most root vegetables.

Plants need the sun to grow healthy, but there are plants that are not too fond of the sun. It is best to group together the ones that love the sun and put them where they can catch most of the sun's rays. Group the ones that love the shade and put them where they can be happy.

In growing runner plants, use strong frames with mesh. Make the area for root crops a little higher to gain maximum depth.

Sample Lay Out for your Square Foot Garden

Row 1: 4 –kale   1 – broccoli   1 –pepper   1 -eggplant
Row 2: 9 -spinach   16 –carrots   16 –arugula   4 - corn
Row 3: 1 –strawberry   1 –sunflower 9 -beats   1 –hot pepper
Row 4: 4 beans   4 –basil   9 – dill   4 – parsley

You can use the sample above as guide. You can interchange the number of crops. You can design a layout that will give the most benefits to the plants (consider plants that love the sun and plants that love the shade).

Plants that can Help Control the Pests or Attract Beneficial Insects

It is best to include a plant or plants that can control the presence of pests. Plants that can attract the beneficial insects can be good addition too. This will make your square foot garden practically survive by itself. Having these plants around does not mean that you have to abandon your garden and never tend to it anymore. These plants only intend to help you safeguard your garden from pests. Proper maintenance and caring still lies within your hands.

Basil is one versatile herb that adds flavor to your dish and repels mosquitoes and flies. The oil in basil is the one that acts as insect repellant. It can give tastier tomatoes if planted alongside the said plant, but will not do well with rue.

Artemisia produces a potent antiseptic that keeps most insects away. The antiseptic does not give off an unpleasant aroma. However, this plant is not suitable for vegetable gardens because it emits botanical poison.

Borage repels cabbage worms and tomato hornworms. It attracts beneficial insects such as wasps and bees to come to your garden. It also adds trace elements that your garden needs.

Catnip can prevent aphids, flea beetles, squash bugs, weevils, ants, and Japanese beetles from approaching your garden.

Chives, like basil, can add flavor to your dish and repel carrot root flies and Japanese beetles.

Bee balm attracts bees to the garden. A swarm of bees is one of the beneficial insects that can help your garden grow.

Onions and cucumbers are best planted together with dill. Predatory wasps and hoverflies are attracted to dill. It can also prevent spider mites and aphids from invading your garden. If you will sprinkle the leaves of dill on your squash in your garden, you will be able to keep squash bugs off your produce.

Dahlias can ward off nematodes and the flowers can create added aesthetic appeal to your garden plus a lively atmosphere.

Garlic has many benefits aside from giving flavor to your dishes and preventing your high blood pressure from causing havoc to your body. It can also ward off aphids, dissuade coddling moths, prevent root maggots and snails, and discourage carrot root fly from approaching your plant. It can be a part of your square foot garden or act as companion plant to prevent the pests from entering your garden.

Hyssop attracts honeybees to visit your garden and bring many benefits to your plants.

Lavender's fresh and aromatic scent can ease the mind and body. Its delicate blue colored blooms are pleasing to the eyes. It is not surprising that it can attract beneficial insects. Lavender can also ward off moths and fleas.

Marigolds are famous for repelling harmful insects. French marigold, in particular, prevents whiteflies from approaching your garden. It can also kill nematodes. Mexican marigolds can prevent the invasion of destructive insects. It can also stop wild rabbits from ruining your garden. Choose the scented variety of marigolds to repel the enemies that you want to stop. Although marigold can prevent bad bugs, it can attract snails and spider mites.

Nasturtiums are effective in fighting off wooly aphids, cucumber beetles, squash bugs, and whiteflies. The flowers of the variety with yellow blooms act as an aphids trap.

Petunias can ward off leafhoppers, tomato worms, aphids, asparagus beetles, and other pests. You can plant petunias throughout the garden or have them in pots and surround the frame of your square foot garden. Arrange them nicely to provide added appeal, and don't overdo it.

Sunflowers can draw aphids and ants toward them and away from other plants in the garden. Sunflowers may look delicate on the outside, but are tough on the inside. They can handle a colony of ants without suffering any damage.

Now that you have your plants and their companion plants, it is time to discover the proper maintenance and care that your garden needs. Give your garden enough attention and it will return the affection a thousand times.

Chapter 5 - Proper Caring and Maintenance

In order to maintain the health of your square foot garden, proper caring and maintenance is required. Your garden will give you a lifetime supply of fresh organic produce if you will give it enough attention. The beauty of SFG, is that it doesn't demand as much from you as a regular garden. You won't have to spend endless hours taking care of your garden, but still, some care is necessary!

Important Things to Consider

It is best to place your square foot garden near your house for ease and convenience especially during harvesting. It is also easier to care for your garden if it is situated near your house.

It is necessary to remove dead leaves and branches to make your garden look fresh and healthy. If you notice that something seems odd with a particular plant, it is best to remove it right away because it might be ill. It could infect other plants if you let it stay longer in the bed.

Use only the right amount of water for your plants. Too little water can lead to wilting or stunned growth. Too much water can turn make the leaves turn yellow.

Never use hose in your square foot garden when you water your plants, especially if you just planted new seeds. There is a huge possibility for the new seeds to get washed away if you use a hose in watering your garden.

Always add compost to your empty square before planting a new crop. Make sure to put a different kind of plant from the last.

Use scissors or garden shears whenever you need to trim your plants or harvest your produce. Do not pull dead plants, cut it from the base to avoid disturbing the root system.

When it becomes too hot, give your plants some shade to keep them fresh and prevent the leaves from turning brown. You can use cheesecloth as cover or shade.

Never step on the soil of your square foot garden. Go around it if you are trying to reach a certain plant. This is why it is important to keep the width at four feet.

It is best to grow compatible plants together and keep your garden healthy. Use some of the plants suggested in the previous chapter, or check out my book on companion planting for more suggestions!

Harvest all your produce as soon as they are ready for the picking. Once you have spent the plant, then it is time to plant a new and different one after adding some of your compost.

Benefits of Cover Crops

Cover crops are legumes or small grains that can protect and improve the condition of the soil. They can also provide water and wind erosion control. They help to improve crop yield and soil tilth.

Cover crops can provide lots of benefits to your square foot garden. There are several plants that can serve as effective cover crops. Rye and oats are two of the cover crops that can be planted a few weeks before the first winter frost. As they grow, they absorb nitrogen. Their roots can prevent soil erosion courtesy of snow melt and winds. Rye can also prevent weeds from invading your garden, just like what buckwheat can do.

Square foot gardening is easy to maintain, efficient, and works well with most plants. You and your family will not only enjoy doing some gardening together, but eating fresh produce right from your own garden.

Conclusion

Thank you again for downloading this book!

I hope this book was able to help you learn more about square foot gardening.

Remember to plan your garden fully, and decide what plants to grow, and where they will be placed. Do your research on your plants, and ensure you know how to care for each one.

Design your garden frame to achieve the aesthetic look you are after, take care of your plants, and most importantly have fun!

The next step is to put this information to use, and begin working on your square foot garden beds!

Also, don't forget to claim your FREE bonus e-book on how to grow tomatoes!
Download your copy at the link below:

http://bit.ly/1ODGQbJ

Finally, if you enjoyed this book, please take the time to share your thoughts and post a review on Amazon. It'd be greatly appreciated!

Thank you and good luck!

www.ingramcontent.com/pod-product-compliance
Lightning Source LLC
LaVergne TN
LVHW021750060526
838200LV00052B/3561